TEX-MEX COOKBOOK

MANY DELICIOUS RECIPES
FROM BOTH SIDES OF THE BORDER

JAMES HERNANDEZ

Table of Contents

Sweet and Spicy Grapefruit Salsa 7

Crispy Mexican Egg Rolls 9

Spicy Chilled Shrimp and Scallops 11

Fried Nopales 13

Salad of Sweet Onion, Corn, and Tomatillo 15

Margarita Fruit Cocktail 17

Jalapeño-Honey Salad 18

Southwestern Tortilla Soup 19

Hearty Corn Chowder 21

Tomato and Chipotle Bisque 23

Cheesy Shrimp Chowder 24

Spanish Rice 26

Mexicali Corn 28

Spiced Potatoes 30

Pico de Gallo 32

Spicy Jalapeño Pesto 33

Ranchero Sauce 35

Salsa with Tomatillo and Cilantro 36

Old-Fashioned Chipotle Corn Bread 37

Hush Puppies 39

Quick Bread with Chorizo 40

Spiced Bolillos	42
Fresh Fish Tacos	44
Red Snapper Veracruz	46
Glazed Tilapia with Guacamole Pesto	48
Classic Crab Rellenos	50
Chicken Enchiladas	52
Tequila-Marinated Chicken	54
Chicken Taquitos	55
Chicken Chimichangas	57
Southwestern Meatloaf	59
Picadillo	61
Easy Beef Migas	63
Sweet and Spicy Burgers	65
Picnic Ribs	67
Adobo-style Pork	69
Slow-Cooked Carnitas	71
Quick Avocado and Chicken Sandwiches	73
Chicken Quesadillas	75
Calcabacita with Ginger	77
Tex-Mex Risotto	78
Veggie-Heavy Taco Salad	80
Curaçao Margaritas	82
Tequila Slammer	83

Rich Mexican Coffee 84

Frozen Bananas with Chocolate and Cayenne 86

Smooth Mango Pie 88

Dulce de Leche 90

Tex-Mex Chocolate Flan 92

Cinnamon-Cherry Enchiladas 94

Sweet and Spicy Grapefruit Salsa

Don't mess with Texas when it comes to grapefruit. For the Lone Star State, the deep ruby reds trademarked "Rio Star" and "Ruby Sweet" are a great source of pride and enjoyment.

Yields 2 cups

Ingredients
2 Ruby Red grapefruits
½ cup finely sliced sweet onion
1 avocado, peeled and diced
1 tablespoon grapefruit juice
2 tablespoons honey
2 teaspoons diced jalapeño pepper
½ teaspoon salt
⅛ teaspoon cayenne pepper

1. Peel grapefruits, removing all the white pith possible. Then cut between the membranes, freeing the grapefruit sections. Place in medium bowl with sliced onion. Prepare avocado and squeeze the grapefruit membranes over them. Add to grapefruit mixture along with honey and remaining ingredients

2. Cover bowl tightly and refrigerate for at least 2 hours before serving. Serve with chips as a dip, or as a side with grilled chicken or steak.

What Are Sweet Onions?
Sweet onions, bred to be sweet and mild, must contain at least 6 percent sugar by weight to earn that label. Other varieties of sweet onions include the famous Vidalia from Georgia, the Maui from Hawaii, the Walla Walla from Washington, and the AmenSweet from Michigan.

Crispy Mexican Egg Rolls

This fusion dish blends the best of Mexican ingredients and bundles them in a convenient Asian-inspired fried wrap. Serve with guacamole topped with fresh cilantro to cut the heat.

Serves 10

Ingredients

1 onion, finely chopped
3 cloves garlic, minced
2 tablespoons olive oil
1 (15-ounce) can black beans, rinsed
2 cups chopped cooked chicken
1 jalapeño pepper, minced
½ teaspoon cumin
1 tablespoon chili powder
⅛ teaspoon cayenne pepper
1 cup shredded Muenster cheese
20 egg roll wrappers
3 cups vegetable oil

1. Preheat oven to 250°F. In heavy skillet, cook onion and garlic in olive oil until tender. Remove from heat and stir in drained black beans, chicken, jalapeño pepper, cumin, chili powder, cayenne pepper, and cheese until blended

2. Place about 3 tablespoons mixture on 1 egg roll wrapper. Moisten edges of wrapper with water. Roll

up wrapper, folding in ends, to form a roll. Repeat with remaining filling and wrappers.

3. In large saucepan, heat oil until a thermometer registers 375°F. Fry egg rolls, two at a time, for 5–8 minutes, turning once, until crisp and golden brown.

4. Remove and drain on paper towels. Keep warm in 250°F oven until all are done. Serve with sour cream, salsa, or ranch salad dressing for dipping.

Make-Ahead Tip
You can make these spicy little egg rolls ahead of time and keep them, tightly covered, in the refrigerator for up to 24 hours. Fry them up as your guests arrive, adding about 2–3 minutes of cooking time because the filling is chilled.

Spicy Chilled Shrimp and Scallops

The prep time is minimal for this saucy seafood medley, but marinating it makes all the difference, so allow yourself enough lead time to allow the flavors to meld before serving.

Serves 6-8

Ingredients

½ cup minced onion
4 cloves garlic, minced
1 tablespoon butter
1 tablespoon oil
1½ pounds large shrimp, deveined and peeled
½ pound bay scallops
1 jalapeño pepper, minced
1 serrano pepper, minced
1 cup chunky salsa
1 tablespoon prepared horseradish
2 tablespoons lemon juice
1 red bell pepper, chopped
¼ cup chopped cilantro

1. In heavy skillet, cook onion and garlic in butter and oil over medium heat until crisp-tender. Add shrimp and scallops; cook and stir until shrimp turn pink and scallops just turn opaque; remove skillet from heat.
2. Add minced peppers, salsa, horseradish, lemon juice, and bell pepper. Pour into serving bowl, cover, and

chill for 3–4 hours to blend flavors. Sprinkle with cilantro and serve.

Fried Nopales

Nopales are the pads of the prickly pear cactus. Tart and reminiscent of the flavor of green bean or asparagus, this delicacy is widely used in Tex-Mex cooking — in salads, soups, casseroles, or grilled. Here you can enjoy it fried.

Serves 8-10

Ingredients

2 precleaned nopales pads
1 egg, beaten
½ cup milk
½ cup yellow cornmeal
½ cup flour
1 tablespoon chili powder
1 teaspoon salt
⅛ teaspoon cayenne pepper
Vegetable oil

1. Rinse the nopales pads and scrub with a vegetable brush to make sure all spines are removed. Using a vegetable peeler, remove any nodules or discolored skin. Cut nopales into ¼" strips.

2. In shallow bowl, combine egg and milk and beat well. In another shallow bowl, combine cornmeal, flour, chili powder, salt, and cayenne pepper and mix well. Dip the nopales strips into egg mixture, then roll in

cornmeal mixture to coat. Place on wire rack to dry for about 30 minutes.

3. Pour 1" of vegetable oil into a heavy saucepan and heat to 375°F. Fry coated nopales for 2–4 minutes until coating is brown and crisp. Drain on paper towels and serve.

Ingredient Substitutions

You can buy nopales already thoroughly cleaned, sliced, and canned in a water or vinegar solution, but they will be difficult to coat and fry. Other vegetables can be used in this recipe, including green beans, small mushrooms, pepper strips, and sliced yellow squash or zucchini.

Salad of Sweet Onion, Corn, and Tomatillo

Tomatillos and ground cherries are often confused for the same fruit, due to the distinctive papery husk that surrounds them. But the latter is much sweeter. If you have access to fresh tomatillos, use them in this recipe.

Serves 4

Ingredients

3 cups corn kernels
2 tablespoons olive oil
3 cloves garlic, chopped
4 tomatoes
1 (10-ounce) can tomatillos, drained
1 tablespoon lime juice
½ cup plain yogurt
1 (4-ounce) can green chiles, drained
½ cup chopped sweet onion
⅓ cup chopped fresh cilantro
9 cups mixed salad greens

1. Preheat oven to 400°F. Combine corn, olive oil, and garlic on baking pan and toss to coat. Roast at 400°F for 12–15 minutes until corn becomes light golden brown around edges. Remove and let cool. Chop tomatoes and place in bowl with corn mixture.

2. In blender container or food processor, place half of the drained tomatillos along with lime juice, yogurt,

green chiles, and sweet onion. Cover and blend or process until mixture is smooth. Stir in fresh cilantro.

3. Chop remaining tomatillos and mix with roasted corn and tomatoes in bowl. Toss with salad greens and drizzle with half of tomatillo dressing. Serve with remaining dressing.

How to Remove Kernels from an Ear of Corn
Firmly hold cob upright on work surface. Using a sharp knife, carefully cut down the cob, removing the kernels but not cutting into the hard portion of the cob. Turn the cob a bit and repeat. After cutting the kernels, use the back of the knife to run down the cob, releasing juices.

Margarita Fruit Cocktail

If you want to spike your cocktail, add a splash of your favorite tequila!

Serves 6

Ingredients

1 cantaloupe

1 honeydew melon

1 pint strawberries

1 pint blueberries

½ pint raspberries

¾ cup frozen margarita mix

¼ cup orange juice

2 tablespoons vegetable oil

2 drops Tabasco sauce

½ teaspoon salt

1. Using melon baller, remove flesh from cantaloupe and honeydew melon; place in serving bowl. Remove stems and slice strawberries and add to bowl. Top with blueberries and raspberries.

2. Thaw margarita mix. In small jar with screw-top lid, combine remaining ingredients and shake well to blend. Pour over fruit and serve.

Jalapeño-Honey Salad

Not to be confused with chicory root, chicory is a bitter specialty green that's also known as endive or Italian dandelion.

Serves 4-6

Ingredients

4 cups butter lettuce

2 cups red lettuce

2 cups chicory

1 (4-ounce) can jalapeño peppers

½ cup sour cream

2 tablespoons honey

2 tablespoons lime juice

½ teaspoon salt

1. Combine lettuces in serving bowl and set aside. In blender or food processor, combine peppers, sour cream, honey, lime juice, and salt. Blend or process until smooth.

2. Pour half of dressing over lettuce mixture and toss gently. Serve remaining dressing on the side..

How to Prepare Greens
To prepare greens, fill a sink with cold water and add the greens. Swish the greens through the water and let stand for 2-3 minutes so any grit falls to the bottom of the sink. Remove the greens, separate if necessary, and lay on kitchen towels. Roll up towels and store in refrigerator for 1-2 hours.

Southwestern Tortilla Soup

Mexican cooking authority Diana Kennedy (author of Essential Cuisines of Mexico, among others) calls classic tortilla soup "a sort of soul food soup." This recipe is a must in your Tex-Mex repertoire.

Serves 6

Ingredients
3 tablespoons vegetable oil
4 (10") flour tortillas
1 onion, chopped
3 cloves garlic, minced
1 green bell pepper, chopped
1 serrano chile, minced
2 tablespoons masa harina
1 (4-ounce) can diced green chiles, undrained
1 (14-ounce) can diced tomatoes, undrained
3 yellow tomatoes, chopped
1 (6-ounce) can tomato paste
3 (14-ounce) cans vegetable broth
2 teaspoons sugar
½ teaspoon pepper
⅛ teaspoon Tabasco sauce

1. In heavy saucepan, heat vegetable oil and fry the tortillas, one at a time, until crisp and golden; set aside to drain on paper towels. In same skillet in same oil, cook onions and garlic until crisp-tender; add bell

pepper and serrano chile and cook 1–2 minutes longer.

2. Add masa harina to saucepan; cook and stir for 2 minutes. Add green chiles, diced tomatoes, yellow tomatoes, tomato paste, vegetable broth, sugar, and pepper. Bring to a boil, then reduce heat, partially cover, and simmer for 15 minutes until slightly thickened. Add Tabasco sauce and stir.

3. Crumble fried tortillas into soup bowls and top with soup; garnish as desired and serve.

Masa Harina Substitution
Masa harina helps to thicken soups and sauces and adds a nutty corn flavor. If you can't find it, you can thicken this soup with the same amount of flour; cook and stir it in the oil and vegetable mixture until the flour turns a very light golden brown.

Hearty Corn Chowder

If you prefer a lighter chowder, substitute whole or low-fat milk for the heavy cream. If you want to give your chowder more kick, add a few dashes of cayenne pepper!

Serves 4-6

Ingredients

1 onion, chopped
2 tablespoons butter
2 cups frozen corn
1 (15-ounce) can creamed corn
2 cups chicken broth
2 tablespoons masa harina
1 cup heavy cream
1 red bell pepper, chopped
1 (4-ounce) can diced chiles
½ teaspoon cumin

1. In heavy saucepan, cook onion in butter until crisp-tender, about 4 minutes. Stir in frozen corn, creamed corn, and half of chicken broth; bring to a boil. Meanwhile, in small saucepan combine remaining chicken broth with masa harina; bring to a boil, stirring constantly.

2. Stir chicken broth and masa harina mixture into onion mixture along with cream, bell pepper, chiles, and

cumin; simmer for 5–8 minutes, stirring frequently, until blended.

Tomato and Chipotle Bisque

Chipotle chiles are smoke-dried jalapeños, which accounts for their mesquite flavor. Serve this hearty soup with warm tortillas or crisp bolillos — a savory Mexican baguette.

Serves 4

Ingredients

4 red tomatoes

2 yellow tomatoes

2 tablespoons butter

½ cup chopped onion

1 chipotle chile in adobo sauce

½ teaspoon dried oregano

1 cup chicken stock

1½ cups half-and-half

½ teaspoon salt

⅛ teaspoon cayenne pepper

1. Peel and seed tomatoes and chop. Melt butter in heavy saucepan and cook tomatoes and onion for 3–4 minutes. Chop chipotle and add to saucepan with oregano and chicken stock. Simmer for 10 minutes, stirring frequently.

2. Mash tomatoes using a potato masher. Stir in half-and-half, salt, and cayenne pepper and heat soup, stirring, until almost simmering.

Cheesy Shrimp Chowder

Offset the richness of this chowder by serving with a salad of crisp greens with lime vinaigrette, chopped avocado, and topped with fresh cilantro.

Serves 6

Ingredients

3 tablespoons butter
1 tablespoon vegetable oil
1 onion, chopped
3 cloves garlic, minced
1 jalapeño pepper, minced
3 carrots, sliced
2 tablespoons flour
1 teaspoon salt
1 chipotle chile in adobo sauce, minced
1½ cups milk
2 cups frozen corn
1 cup frozen hash brown potatoes
1 pound raw shrimp
1 (8-ounce) package cream cheese
1½ cups shredded Muenster cheese

1. In large saucepan, melt butter and oil over medium heat. Cook onion, garlic, jalapeño pepper, and carrots until crisp-tender, about 4–5 minutes. Add flour and salt; cook and stir until bubbly.

2. Stir in chipotle and milk and bring just to a simmer. Add corn and potatoes and bring back to a simmer. Add shrimp and bring to a simmer; cook for 4–5 minutes until shrimp just begin to curl and turn pink.

3. Cut cream cheese into cubes and add to chowder; cook and stir for a few minutes until cheese melts. Add Muenster cheese, stir, and serve.

Frozen Vegetables

Don't be afraid to use frozen vegetables. Since the vegetables are picked, processed, and frozen within hours, the quality is very high. Frozen peas, especially, are almost always better than fresh, unless you have your own garden. Stock up on frozen vegetables and you can whip up a chowder or soup in minutes.

Spanish Rice

Rice cooked with onions, garlic, peppers, and tomatoes is a fabulous side dish — you can serve it with everything from grilled steak to chicken soup. In Spanish-speaking cultures, this mixture is called a sofrito.

Serves 6

Ingredients

2 tablespoons vegetable oil
1 onion, chopped
3 cloves garlic, minced
1 jalapeño pepper, minced
1½ cups Texmati rice
2½ cups water
1 (14-ounce) can diced tomatoes, undrained
1 tablespoon chili powder
½ teaspoon cumin
½ teaspoon salt
Dash pepper

1. In large saucepan, heat vegetable oil over medium heat and cook onion, garlic, and pepper until crisp-tender. Add rice; cook and stir for 5–8 minutes until rice becomes opaque.

2. Stir in remaining ingredients and bring to a boil. Cover, reduce heat, and simmer for 20–30 minutes or

until rice is tender. Let stand off heat for 5 minutes. Fluff with fork and serve.

Mexicali Corn

A cheesy casserole that features classic Mexican flavors. A great option to bring to a potluck or serve at brunch along with spicy seasoned eggs and tortillas because you can make it well in advance.

Serves 8

Ingredients

¼ cup butter
3 tablespoons vegetable oil
1 onion, chopped
1 green bell pepper, chopped
2 cups frozen corn
1 (16-ounce) can creamed corn
1 jalapeño pepper, minced
1 (8-ounce) package corn muffin mix
2 eggs, beaten
1 cup sour cream
⅓ cup milk
1 cup shredded pepper jack cheese
½ cup shredded Colby cheese
¼ cup grated cotija or Parmesan cheese

1. Preheat oven to 350°F. Grease a 2½-quart baking dish and set aside. In heavy skillet, melt butter with oil and sauté onion and green bell pepper until crisp-tender, about 4 minutes. Stir in frozen corn; cook and stir until corn is thawed, 3–4 minutes longer.

2. Stir in remaining ingredients except cotija or Parmesan cheese [and mix well until blended. Pour into prepared pan. Sprinkle with cotija or Parmesan cheese and bake at 350°F for 40–50 minutes or until casserole is set and golden brown. Serve immediately.

Spiced Potatoes

Hot salt can be found at specialty stores or online and consists of a blend of dried hot peppers mixed with kosher salt. Don't omit it when preparing these simple but tasty roasted potatoes — it helps turn up the heat!

Serves 6

Ingredients

2 pounds small red potatoes

3 tablespoons vegetable oil

3 cloves garlic, minced

1 teaspoon hot salt

⅛ teaspoon pepper

½ teaspoon cumin

3 chipotle chiles in adobo sauce

3 tablespoons adobo sauce

1. Preheat oven to 400°F. Cut each potato into quarters and toss with vegetable oil in roasting pan. Sprinkle with garlic, hot salt, pepper, and cumin, and toss again. Bake at 400°F for 30 minutes.

2. Meanwhile, chop chipotle. Remove pan from oven and sprinkle chiles over potatoes. Return to oven and bake 10 minutes longer. Remove pan from oven and drizzle with adobo sauce.

3. Return to oven and bake 10–15 minutes longer until potatoes are golden and crisp, but tender when tested with fork.

Pico de Gallo

This citrusy salsa fresca is so juicy and sweet, it will go before you run out of tortilla chips to serve it on!

Yields 2 cups

Ingredients

3 ripe red tomatoes

2 ripe golden tomatoes

½ sweet onion

2 tablespoons lemon juice

1 tablespoon orange juice

1 jalapeño pepper

¼ cup chopped fresh parsley

1 teaspoon salt

⅛ teaspoon cayenne pepper

1. Cut tomatoes in half, seed them, then cut into small pieces. Dice onion and combine with tomatoes in a medium bowl. Sprinkle with lemon and orange juice.

2. Seed and dice jalapeño pepper. Add to tomato mixture along with parsley. Sprinkle with salt and cayenne pepper and toss to coat. Cover and chill for 1–2 hours to blend flavors, or serve immediately. Store leftovers, covered, in refrigerator.

Spicy Jalapeño Pesto

A Tex-Mex take on Italian pesto celebrates the icon flavors of the region, with roasted pepitas taking the place of pine nuts, cilantro standing in for basil, and lime in lieu of lemon. This freezes well, so make a large batch and store for later.

Yields 2 cups

Ingredients

½ cup pumpkin seeds
1 tablespoon vegetable oil
½ cup chopped onion
2 cloves garlic, minced
5 jalapeño peppers
1 cup cilantro leaves
1 cup flat leaf parsley
2 tablespoons lime juice
½ teaspoon salt
¼ teaspoon pepper
½ cup olive oil
⅓ cup grated Manchego or Romano cheese

1. In small skillet, toast pumpkin seeds over medium heat until light brown and fragrant. Remove to kitchen towel to cool. In same skillet, heat vegetable oil and sauté onion and garlic until tender. Remove to blender or food processor bowl.

2. Add cooled seeds, jalapeños, cilantro, parsley, lime juice, salt, and pepper and blend or process until finely chopped. With motor running, add olive oil in a thin stream until a paste forms. Remove to bowl and stir in cheese.

3. Press plastic wrap onto surface and refrigerate up to 2 days, or freeze up to 3 months.

Ingredient Substitutions
Other nuts can be substituted for pumpkin seeds. Peanuts, pine nuts, and slivered almonds have about the same texture and similar flavor. For a richer flavor, use pecans or cashews. Remember to let all nuts cool thoroughly after roasting and before chopping or processing, or they will be soggy.

Ranchero Sauce

A staple sauce to add to eggs, potatoes, or grilled meat, this is an indispensible addition to your Tex-Mex recipe library.

Yields 2 cups

Ingredients
1 tablespoon vegetable oil
1 onion, chopped
2 cloves garlic, minced
1 green bell pepper, chopped
2 jalapeño peppers, minced
1 (14-ounce) can fire-roasted chopped tomatoes
3 tablespoons tomato paste
1 tablespoon chili powder
1 teaspoon salt
¼ teaspoon pepper

1. Heat oil in heavy skillet over medium heat. Cook onion and garlic in oil for 4–5 minutes, stirring frequently, until crisp-tender. Add bell pepper, jalapeños, chopped tomatoes with their liquid, tomato paste, chili powder, salt, and pepper.
2. Bring to a boil, then cover pan, reduce heat, and simmer for 15–20 minutes until sauce thickens.

3. Cool the sauce and store, covered, in the refrigerator up to 3 days, or freeze for longer storage. Reheat before use.

Salsa with Tomatillo and Cilantro

When shopping for tomatillos, look for smaller fruits whose husks are fresh-looking and light brown. Larger tomatillos aren't as sweet and a shriveled, dried husk indicates it's old.

Yields 2 cups

Ingredients
1 pint fresh tomatillos
1 tablespoon vegetable oil
1 onion, chopped
2 cloves garlic, minced
1 minced serrano chile
½ cup chopped cilantro
1 teaspoon salt
⅛ teaspoon pepper
⅛ teaspoon cayenne pepper

1. Remove husks from tomatillos and rinse. Dry well and coarsely chop. Heat vegetable oil in heavy saucepan and sauté onion and garlic until crisp-tender. Add chopped tomatillos and cook for 2–3 minutes until tomatillos begin to soften.

2. Remove from heat and add remaining ingredients. Cool to room temperature, then place in container, cover, and refrigerate up to 4 days or freeze up to 3 months.

Old-Fashioned Chipotle Corn Bread

Smoky chipotles and creamy queso blanco elevate this corn bread from the standard category into the scrumptious category! Use this savory bread to sop up a bowl of hearty chili.

Serves 8

Ingredients
2 chipotle peppers in adobo sauce, drained
1½ cups flour
1 cup yellow cornmeal
1 tablespoon baking powder
½ teaspoon salt
¼ cup sugar
2 eggs
½ cup milk
½ cup plain yogurt
⅓ cup vegetable oil
1 cup crumbled queso blanco

1. Preheat oven to 400°F. Grease a 9" square pan with solid shortening or nonstick baking spray and set aside. Finely chop chipotle peppers and set aside.

2. In large bowl, combine flour, cornmeal, baking powder, salt, and sugar and blend well. In small bowl, combine eggs, milk, yogurt, and oil and mix until blended. Add to dry ingredients along with chipotle peppers and cheese and stir just until blended.

3. Pour into prepared pan; bake at 400°F for 25–30 minutes or until bread is firm to the touch and light golden brown. Serve warm.

Colored Cornmeal
Corn bread can be made with yellow cornmeal, red cornmeal, white cornmeal, or even blue cornmeal. All of it tastes about the same; the difference will be in the appearance of the finished product, although red cornmeal may have ground chiles added. If not, red cornmeal is made from a special variety of red corn that is sweeter than white or yellow.

Hush Puppies

Hush puppies were first made in the Deep South when fishermen would fry extra batter in little round balls and throw them to their hunting dogs, saying "Hush, puppies!"

Yields 24

Ingredients

1 cup yellow cornmeal

1 cup flour

1 teaspoon baking powder

½ teaspoon baking soda

½ teaspoon smoked paprika

⅓ cup buttermilk

2 eggs

½ cup chopped sweet onion

4 cups vegetable oil

1. In large bowl, combine cornmeal, flour, baking powder, baking soda, and paprika and mix well. In medium bowl, combine buttermilk, eggs, and sweet onion and beat well. Mix dry and wet ingredients together just until blended.

2. Heat oil in large heavy saucepan to 375°F. Drop batter by spoonfuls into hot oil, about five or six at a time, and fry until golden brown. Remove and drain on paper towels. Serve hot.

Quick Bread with Chorizo

In Mexico, chorizo is a popular food, found on top of pizzas, mixed with beans and stuffed into a torta, combined with cheese, and the list goes on …. Here you get the spicy taste of pork sausage infused into a rich baked bread.

Yields 1 loaf

Ingredients

¼ pound chorizo sausage
½ cup chopped red bell pepper
3 green onions, chopped
1¾ cups flour
1 tablespoon sugar
2 teaspoons baking powder
½ teaspoon baking soda
½ teaspoon salt
⅛ teaspoon cayenne pepper
1 egg
¾ cup buttermilk
1 tablespoon honey
¼ cup vegetable oil
1 cup shredded Cheddar cheese

1. Preheat oven to 400°F. Spray 9" × 5" loaf pan with nonstick baking spray and set aside. In heavy skillet, cook chorizo sausage with red bell pepper until sausage is thoroughly cooked, stirring to break up

sausage. Drain well, remove from heat, stir in green onions, and cool.

2. In large bowl, combine flour, sugar, baking powder and soda, salt, and cayenne pepper and stir to combine. In small bowl, combine egg, buttermilk, honey, and vegetable oil and beat until combined. Add to dry ingredients and stir just until combined. Add cheese along with chorizo mixture and stir gently.

3. Pour batter into prepared pan and bake at 400°F for 30–40 minutes until bread is deep golden brown and bread pulls away from edges of pan. Remove from pan and cool slightly on wire rack. Cut into thick slices and serve warm.

How to Make Quick Bread
For the best quick breads, be sure to mix the dry and wet ingredients separately, and when you combine them, stir just until the dry ingredients disappear. Overmixing will result in a tough loaf. And don't worry about the crack that develops in the center — that's the way quick breads are supposed to look!

Spiced Bolillos

Bolillos, or Mexican hard rolls, really take a back seat to tortillas in the Tex-Mex kitchen, but they are delicious. The sweet, cinnamon flavor of these makes them a perfect way to start the day.

Yields 24

Ingredients

1 package active dry yeast
¼ cup warm water
1 teaspoon sugar
½ cup milk
1 tablespoon butter
1 cup water
2 tablespoons sugar
½ teaspoon salt
¼ teaspoon cinnamon
6 cups bread flour
1 egg white

1. In small bowl, combine yeast, ¼ cup warm water, and 1 teaspoon sugar. Let stand until bubbly. Meanwhile, combine milk, butter, 1 cup water, sugar, and salt in heavy saucepan over medium heat until butter melts. Remove and let cool to lukewarm.

2. In large mixing bowl, combine cooled milk mixture, yeast mixture, cinnamon, and 2 cups flour; beat at medium speed for 1 minute. Gradually add remaining

flour until dough is too stiff to beat. Remove to a flour-dusted work surface and knead in enough of the remaining flour to make smooth and elastic dough.

3. Place dough in a greased bowl, turning to grease top. Cover and let rise in warm place until doubled in size, about 1 hour. Punch down dough and turn onto floured work surface; cover with bowl and let sit for 10 minutes.

4. Divide dough into 24 pieces and form into football shapes. Place on greased baking sheets, cover, and let rise until doubled, 30–40 minutes. Preheat oven to 375°F. In small bowl, beat egg white until frothy; gently brush over rolls. Bake at 375°F for 20–30 minutes or until rolls are light golden brown and sound hollow when tapped on bottom. Cool completely on wire racks.

How to Freeze Rolls

These rolls — and all yeast breads — freeze very well. Make sure they are completely cooled, then package into freezer bags, label well, seal, and freeze up to 3 months. To thaw, let stand, uncovered, at room temperature for about $1^1/_2$ hours. You can reheat the rolls in the microwave oven.

Fresh Fish Tacos

A popular recipe in Texas's Gulf Coast, you can't beat the fresh flavors of fish seasoned with cumin and chili powder.

Serves 4-6

Ingredients

1 pound red snapper fillets
3 tablespoons cornmeal
1 tablespoon flour
½ teaspoon salt
2 teaspoons chili powder
¼ teaspoon cumin
¼ teaspoon pepper
1 egg, beaten
3 tablespoons heavy cream
1 cup cilantro, chopped
⅓ cup sour cream
¼ cup olive oil
1 avocado
1 tablespoon lime juice
1 (15-ounce) can cannelloni beans, rinsed
2 cups shredded lettuce
1 cup shredded Monterey jack cheese
8 crisp taco shells, heated

1. Cut fish fillets into 1" pieces and set aside. In shallow bowl, combine cornmeal, flour, salt, chili powder,

cumin, and pepper and mix well. In another shallow bowl, combine egg and cream and beat until combined. Dip fish pieces into egg mixture, then roll in cornmeal mixture to coat; set on wire rack.

2. In small bowl, combine cilantro and sour cream; blend well, cover, and place in refrigerator. Heat olive oil in heavy skillet over medium heat. Cook coated fish pieces in oil for 3–4 minutes, turning once, until golden brown. Peel and dice avocado and sprinkle with lime juice.

3. Make tacos by filling heated taco shells with fish, beans, avocado, cilantro sauce, lettuce, and cheese.

Red Snapper Veracruz

So easy, and so delicious! This casserole gives you a healthy main course best served over yellow rice with a simple spinach salad.

Serves 6

Ingredients

6 (6-ounce) red snapper fillets
2 tablespoons lime juice
1 tablespoon chili powder
1 teaspoon salt
2 tablespoons butter
1 tablespoon oil
1 onion, sliced
4 cloves garlic, minced
1 serrano chile, minced
4 tomatoes, seeded and diced
2 tablespoons tomato paste
½ teaspoon dried oregano
2 tablespoons tequila
⅓ cup sliced green olives
1 tablespoon capers
Salt and pepper to taste
¼ cup chopped cilantro
1 avocado, sliced

1. Preheat oven to 350°F. Place red snapper in glass baking dish in single layer; sprinkle with lime juice, chili powder, and salt; set aside.

2. In heavy skillet, melt butter and oil over medium heat and cook onion, garlic, and serrano chile until crisp-tender, about 4–5 minutes. Add tomatoes, tomato paste, oregano, and tequila; simmer for 5–10 minutes over medium heat. Stir in olives, capers, and salt and pepper to taste; pour over red snapper in baking dish.

3. Bake at 350°F for 12–18 minutes or until fish flakes when tested with fork. Sprinkle fish with cilantro and garnish with avocado; serve immediately.

Glazed Tilapia with Guacamole Pesto

The creamy freshness of the guacamole pesto is a perfect foil for the spicy and saucy grilled tilapia. When it comes together it's like a fiesta in your mouth!

Serves 4

Ingredients

1 avocado
2 tablespoons lemon juice
¼ cup chopped cilantro
¼ cup crumbled queso fresco
2 tablespoons pine nuts
2 tablespoons mayonnaise
2 tablespoons adobo sauce
4 tilapia fillets

1. Peel avocado and cut into chunks. Place in blender or food processor with lemon juice, cilantro, queso fresco, and pine nuts. Blend or process until mixture is smooth. Meanwhile, prepare and preheat grill.

2. Combine mayonnaise and adobo sauce in small bowl. Place fish fillets on grill and brush with mayonnaise mixture. Cover and cook for 2–3 minutes, then turn fish, brush with remaining mayonnaise mixture, cover grill, and cook for about 3 minutes until fish flakes easily. Serve with avocado pesto.

Grill Baskets

There are many accessories for your gas or charcoal grill. Grill baskets are a great way to cook smaller pieces of vegetables or meat, and to cook fragile foods such as fish fillets and shrimp. Brush the basket lightly with oil and add the food, then cook on the grill, using an oven mitt to handle the basket.

Classic Crab Rellenos

Milder in flavor and larger than other chiles, poblanos are the natural choice for any stuffed dish, "rellenos" style.

Serves 6

Ingredients

6 poblano chiles
1½ cups lump crabmeat
2 tablespoons butter
½ cup chopped onion
½ cup chopped yellow squash
1 clove garlic, minced
1 tomato, seeded and chopped
2 tablespoons lemon juice
1½ cups shredded pepper jack cheese
2 tablespoons flour
4 eggs, separated
¼ cup flour
1 teaspoon salt
2 cups vegetable oil

1. Roast poblano chiles under a broiler or over a gas flame until skin is charred. Place in paper bag and let steam for 10 minutes. Peel peppers, cut a slit in the side, and remove membranes and seeds.
2. Pick over crabmeat, getting rid of cartilage and shell. In heavy skillet, melt butter over medium heat and

cook onion until crisp-tender. Add squash, garlic, tomato, and lemon juice; cook and stir for 3–4 minutes. Stir in crabmeat, then remove pan from heat and let it cool for 30 minutes.

3. Stuff peppers with crab mixture and 2 tablespoons pepper jack cheese. Sprinkle with 2 tablespoons flour and shake off excess. In medium bowl, beat egg whites until stiff. In another medium bowl, beat egg yolks with ¼ cup flour, and salt; fold into egg whites.

4. Heat vegetable oil to 350°F in deep heavy skillet. Dip stuffed chiles, one at a time, into egg batter and gently lower into oil. Fry for 2–4 minutes on each side until golden brown. Drain on kitchen or paper towels and serve with salsa.

About Crabmeat
Bulk crabmeat purchased frozen has been processed and frozen within hours of the catch. Lump crabmeat is the most expensive, since it comes from the body of the crab. Backfin and flake consist of smaller pieces that come from the leg and other body parts. Crab should smell fresh and be white, colored with a bit of brown or red.

Chicken Enchiladas

Many Tex-Mex dishes feature lots of green vegetables — green bell peppers, poblanos, tomatillos — hence "verde." These tasty enchiladas rival anything you could get while eating out.

Serves 8

Ingredients
3 whole chicken breasts
2 tablespoons vegetable oil
1 teaspoon salt
⅛ teaspoon white pepper
2 poblano chiles
2 green bell peppers
1 cup tomatillos, husks removed
½ cup heavy cream
2 jalapeño peppers, diced
1 onion, chopped
3 cloves garlic, minced
1 (8-ounce) package cream cheese, softened
2 green onions, chopped
2 cups shredded Monterey jack cheese
12 (6") corn tortillas
¼ cup chopped cilantro

1. Preheat oven to 375°F. Place chicken breasts on cookie sheet and drizzle with olive oil; sprinkle with salt and pepper. Bake at 375°F for 25–30 minutes or until

chicken is thoroughly cooked. Remove from oven and set aside until cool enough to handle. Shred chicken, discarding skin and bones.

2. Set oven to broil. Place poblano chiles and green bell peppers on baking sheet and broil 4" from heat source until blackened, turning frequently. Remove from oven and place in a paper bag; seal bag and let stand for 10 minutes. Remove skin from peppers by gently rubbing with paper towel; cut open and remove membranes and seeds.

3. Place roasted chiles and peppers in blender or food processor along with tomatillos, cream, jalapeño pepper, onion, and garlic. Blend or process until smooth.

4. In medium bowl, combine shredded chicken with cream cheese, green onion, 1 cup Monterey jack cheese, the cilantro, and 1 cup of the blended pepper sauce. Fill corn tortillas with this mixture and place in 13" × 9" baking dish. Pour remaining green sauce over all and sprinkle with remaining Monterey jack cheese. Bake at 375°F for 35–45 minutes or until sauce is bubbling and cheese melts and begins to brown.

Make Your Own Chicken Broth
You can freeze the skin and bones of cooked chicken breasts to make broth. When you accumulate a few pounds of the skin and bones, place in cold water to cover with onion, garlic, and celery and simmer for 2–3 hours. Freeze broth in ice cube trays and use as desired.

Tequila-Marinated Chicken

You couldn't find a simpler weekday meal; prep in the morning and grill in the evening.

Serves 4

Ingredients

¼ cup tequila

¼ cup lime juice

2 tablespoons adobo sauce

1 teaspoon sugar

1 teaspoon salt

⅛ teaspoon cayenne pepper

4 cloves garlic, minced

4 chicken breasts

1. In large bowl, combine all ingredients except chicken breasts and mix well. Add chicken and turn to coat. Cover and refrigerate for 2–4 hours.

2. Prepare and heat grill. Remove chicken from marinade and place, skin side down, on grill. Cover and cook for 10 minutes. Turn chicken, cover again, and cook for 10–20 minutes or until chicken is thoroughly cooked. Discard remaining marinade.

Chicken Taquitos

A taquito is a cross between a taco and a burrito. Filled tortillas are rolled up and fried until crisp; the open ends are reminiscent of tacos. Be sure to carefully tip them from side to side to drain well when you remove them from the oil.

Serves 6

Ingredients

1 pound chicken breasts
1 tablespoon butter
1 onion, chopped
3 cloves garlic, minced
1 chipotle chile, minced
½ teaspoon salt
⅛ teaspoon pepper
¼ cup chopped cilantro
12 corn tortillas, warmed
1½ cups shredded Cheddar cheese
2 cups vegetable oil

1. Cut chicken into 1" chunks and brown in butter for 4–5 minutes. Add onion, garlic, and chipotle chile; cook and stir until chicken is thoroughly cooked, about 5 minutes longer. Season with salt and pepper and stir in cilantro. Using two forks, shred chicken finely and stir filling well.

2. Place two tablespoons chicken filling on each tortilla and top with some cheese. Roll up tightly and fasten with toothpicks. In heavy skillet, heat oil to 375°F and fry taquitos, two or three at a time, until very crisp. Drain on paper towels and serve.

Chicken Chimichangas

This classic menu item at Texas roadhouse restaurants is as fun to eat as it is to say! Serve with ample sides for dipping: sour cream, guacamole, salsa verde, and pico de gallo.

Serves 6

Ingredients

2 tablespoons butter
1 onion, chopped
3 cloves garlic, minced
1 green bell pepper, chopped
1 serrano chile, minced
2 cups cooked chopped chicken
2 plum tomatoes, seeded and chopped
½ teaspoon cumin
1 teaspoon salt
⅛ teaspoon pepper
8 (8") flour tortillas
2 cups vegetable oil

1. In heavy skillet, heat butter and add onion and garlic; cook and stir over medium heat until crisp-tender. Add bell pepper, serrano chile, chicken, and tomatoes; season with cumin, salt, and pepper. Cook and stir for 2–3 minutes. Cool for 30 minutes.

2. Place ¼ cup filling on each tortilla and fold tortilla around filling, tucking in sides. Heat oil in heavy

skillet over medium heat to 375°F and fry chimichangas, two at a time, for 2–4 minutes on each side until brown and crisp. Drain well on paper towels before serving.

Southwestern Meatloaf

Crushed tortilla chips lend an extra note of body to this spicy and sweet meatloaf. Serve with a side of Mexicali Corn and spread with Spicy Jalapeño Pesto for an unforgettable comfort meal.

Serves 6

Ingredients

1 cup finely crushed tortilla chips
1 tablespoon chili powder
½ teaspoon dried oregano
⅛ teaspoon pepper
¼ cup buttermilk
1 egg
¼ cup salsa
2 tablespoons chopped cilantro
1 pound ground beef
½ pound pork sausage
¼ cup ketchup
1 tablespoon mustard
½ teaspoon Tabasco sauce

1. Preheat oven to 350°F. In large bowl, combine crushed tortilla chips, chili powder, oregano, pepper, buttermilk, egg, salsa, and cilantro and mix well until blended.

2. Add beef and sausage to buttermilk mixture and mix gently using hands. Do not overwork! Shape into oval

loaf and place on broiler pan. In small bowl, combine ketchup, mustard, and Tabasco sauce and spread over loaf.

3. Bake at 350°F for 55–65 minutes or until meat thermometer inserted in center registers 165°F. Remove from oven, cover with foil, and let stand for 10 minutes before slicing.

Meatloaf Tips
The critical steps to making meatloaf are to make sure you do not overwork the meat, as this compacts the mixture and makes the meatloaf tough, and to let the meatloaf stand, covered with foil, for about 10 minutes after cooking so the juices can redistribute.

Picadillo

A dish popular in most Latin American countries, picadillo is a spicy beef mixture made with ground beef, raisins, olives, and almonds. It's filling and tastes better the second and third day, so make enough for leftovers.

Serves 8

Ingredients

1 pound ground beef
1 onion, chopped
3 cloves garlic, minced
1 (14-ounce) can diced tomatoes with green chiles, undrained
3 tablespoons tomato paste
½ cup beef broth
⅓ cup raisins
1 tablespoon chili powder
½ teaspoon salt
⅛ teaspoon cayenne pepper
1 tablespoon vinegar
⅛ teaspoon cinnamon
¼ cup sliced pimento-stuffed green olives
¼ cup slivered almonds

1. In heavy skillet, brown ground beef with onion and garlic until beef is no longer pink, stirring frequently to break up meat. Drain well.

2. Add remaining ingredients, stir, and simmer over low heat for 15–20 minutes to blend flavors. Serve with soft tacos, warmed tortillas, or hot cooked rice.

Easy Beef Migas

Corn chips are a classic Texas treat not common in Mexico. In this layered casserole, they take the place of pasta; the chips soften slightly as the casserole bakes but retain a bit of crunch.

Serves 4-6

Ingredients
1 pound ground beef
1 onion, chopped
2 cloves garlic, minced
1 (8-ounce) can tomato sauce
1 (14-ounce) can diced tomatoes with green chiles, undrained
2 tablespoons taco seasoning mix (any brand)
2 cups frozen corn
1 (15-ounce) can pinto beans, drained
2 jalapeño peppers, minced
½ cup garlic-stuffed green olive slices
1 (8-ounce) bag corn chips
1½ cups shredded Colby cheese

1. Preheat oven to 375°F. In heavy skillet, cook ground beef, onion, and garlic until beef is browned, stirring to break up meat. Drain well if necessary. Stir in tomato sauce, diced tomatoes, and taco seasoning mix; stir well. Simmer over medium heat for 5 minutes.

2. Stir in corn, pinto beans, jalapeño pepper, and olives. In 2-quart casserole, layer one-third beef mixture with

one-third of the chips. Repeat layers, ending with beef mixture. Sprinkle cheese over the top.

3. Bake at 375°F for 25–35 minutes or until cheese melts and casserole bubbles around the edge. Top with sour cream, salsa, and chopped avocado and serve.

More Toppings
You can put out more toppings if you'd like. Shredded lettuce, chopped fresh tomatoes, different types of shredded cheese, minced jalapeño or serrano chiles, or pico de gallo and salsa verde are all good with the bean and beef combination in this dish.

Sweet and Spicy Burgers

Anaheim chiles are milder chiles that hail from New Mexico; if you can't find them, you can substitute with a poblano for similar flavor and heat.

Serves 6

Ingredients

2 Anaheim chiles
1½ pounds ground beef
½ cup tortilla chip crumbs
¼ cup chopped sweet onion
¼ teaspoon cayenne pepper
6 slices pepper jack cheese
6 toasted whole wheat hamburger buns
1 cup salsa
½ cup sour cream

1. Broil Anaheim chiles 4–6" from heat, turning frequently, until charred all over. Place in paper bag and let steam for 10 minutes. Remove skin using paper towel or kitchen towel. Chop one of the peppers and slice the other.

2. In large bowl, combine chopped pepper, ground beef, tortilla chip crumbs, onion, and cayenne pepper; mix gently but thoroughly. Form into 6 hamburgers.

3. Grill hamburgers for 10–14 minutes, turning once, until meat is thoroughly cooked and instant-read thermometer registers 165°F. Top with pepper jack cheese and a few pepper slices, cover grill, and heat for 2–3 minutes to melt cheese. Serve on toasted buns with salsa and sour cream.

Ingredient Substitution
Just about any burger recipe can be made with ground turkey. There are two kinds of ground turkey: regular, which contains dark and white meat, and ground turkey breast, which is just white meat. Use regular for most burgers because it has a bit more fat and the burgers will be moister.

Picnic Ribs

Texans love their ribs, so here's the requisite recipe! Best enjoyed outside, under a shady tree with friends, these ribs are so lick-smacking good you'll want to have several napkins and wet naps available for sticky hands.

Serves 6-8

Ingredients

1 cup ketchup
½ cup chicken broth
2 tablespoons lime juice
2 tablespoons Worcestershire sauce
3 tablespoons brown sugar
½ cup diced onion
1 teaspoon salt
2 tablespoons chile powder
½ teaspoon celery salt
¼ teaspoon cayenne pepper
4 pounds pork baby back ribs

1. In heavy saucepan, combine all ingredients except ribs and bring to a boil. Reduce heat and simmer for 20 minutes to blend flavors. Let cool completely. Place ribs on large rectangles of heavy-duty foil and pour half of sauce over them. Wrap ribs in foil and refrigerate overnight.

2. Preheat oven to 300°F. Place ribs, still wrapped in foil, in baking pan and bake at 300°F for 2 hours. Uncover, add more sauce, and bake for 30–45 minutes longer until ribs are very tender. Serve with additional reheated sauce.

3. To grill ribs, first bake them as directed for 2 hours. Then place over medium coals and grill, covered, for 30–45 minutes, basting with sauce, until very tender.

Cookout Safety
After you're done grilling with charcoal, let the coals cool completely. Do not transfer warm or hot coals to another container or you risk starting a fire. Place the grill on a nonflammable surface, such as concrete or asphalt, and keep an eye on it until everything has completely cooled.

Adobo-style Pork

Adobo refers to a marinade given to a meat; in this case, it's a blend of chili peppers, garlic, and vinegar. Texmati rice is a white rice that combines the qualities of basmati and long grain rice. It has a nutty flavor.

Serves 8

Ingredients

2-pound boneless pork shoulder roast
¼ cup apple cider vinegar
¼ cup soy sauce
¼ cup adobo sauce
½ cup tomato sauce
1 cup water
1 onion, chopped
3 garlic cloves, minced
1 jalapeño pepper, minced
¼ teaspoon crushed red pepper flakes
3 chipotle chiles in adobo sauce, minced
3 tablespoons olive oil
3 cups cooked Texmati rice

1. Trim excess fat from pork and cut into 2" cubes. Combine in large bowl with vinegar, soy sauce, adobo sauce, and tomato sauce, and refrigerate overnight.

2. The next day, pour pork and marinade into heavy saucepan and add water, onion, garlic, jalapeño

pepper, red pepper flakes, and chipotle chiles; bring to a boil. Reduce heat, cover, and simmer pork for 35–45 minutes until pork and onions are very tender.

3. In heavy skillet, heat olive oil over medium heat. With a slotted spoon or strainer, remove pork from adobo sauce and add to pan. Cook until cubes are brown, about 10 minutes, stirring frequently. Add sauce to skillet with pork and bring to a simmer. Serve immediately with hot cooked rice.

Texmati and Basmati Rice
Texmati rice is a long-grain rice grown in Texas that is a variety of the Basmati rice used in Indian cooking. It has a tender texture and smells like popcorn when it's cooking. Let it stand, covered, for 5 minutes after it has finished cooking so the grains will be separate and fluffy.

Slow-Cooked Carnitas

Carnitas refers to slow-roasted meat that's then cooked until crisp. It's just as common to see beef in a carnitas recipe, but this one favors flavorful pork.

Serves 8-10

Ingredients

4-pound pork roast
2 teaspoons salt
¼ teaspoon pepper
1 teaspoon cumin
1 onion, chopped
5 cloves garlic, chopped
½ cup chicken broth

1. Sprinkle roast with salt, pepper, and cumin, and place in a 4- to 6-quart crockpot. Surround with onions and garlic and pour chicken broth over all. Cover and cook on low for 8–9 hours until pork is very tender.

2. Preheat oven to 400°F. Remove pork from crockpot and place in large baking pan. Using two forks, shred meat. Take 1 cup of pan juices from the crockpot and mix into pork.

3. Bake at 400°F for 15–20 minutes or until pork is crisp on top. Stir pork mixture thoroughly and bake for 15–20 minutes longer or until pork is again crisp on top.

Serve with crisp tacos, flour or corn tortillas, and lots of salsa.

Make It Spicy
Traditionally, carnitas is cooked without chili powder or fresh or dried chiles. However, you can certainly add some to the crockpot to help flavor the pork as it cooks. A chipotle pepper packed in adobo sauce, minced, would be delicious.

Quick Avocado and Chicken Sandwiches

These grilled chicken sandwiches are a perfect lunch option for when you want something that comes together quickly.

Serves 4

Ingredients

4 boneless, skinless chicken breasts
1 tablespoon adobo sauce
1 tablespoon chili powder
½ teaspoon salt
⅛ teaspoon cayenne pepper
2 avocados
2 tablespoons lime juice
¼ cup mayonnaise
8 slices whole wheat bread, toasted
4 slices Monterey jack cheese

1. Place chicken breasts between pieces of waxed paper and flatten slightly with rolling pin. In small bowl, combine adobo sauce, chili powder, salt, and cayenne pepper; rub over both sides of chicken breasts. Heat dual-contact grill; cook chicken, one at a time, for 4–5 minutes or until thoroughly cooked. Cover and set aside.

2. Peel avocados; slice one thinly, sprinkle with half of lime juice, and set aside. Mash second avocado with remaining lime juice and mayonnaise. Toast bread

and top half of bread with cheese. Spread mayonnaise mixture on one side of remaining bread slices. Slice chicken breasts into thin strips and add to sandwich; top with sliced avocados and remaining toast; serve immediately.

Chicken Quesadillas

A delicious crispy Mexican version of grilled cheese, with this recipe adjust the fillings to include beef, vegetables, or just cheese if you wish. Go with what you're craving and above all, enjoy!

Serves 4-6

Ingredients

2 boneless, skinless chicken breasts
1 tablespoon chili powder
½ teaspoon salt
⅛ teaspoon pepper
1 tablespoon vegetable oil
1½ cups shredded Muenster cheese
½ cup shredded Cheddar cheese
2 jalapeño peppers, minced
8 (10") flour tortillas

1. Cut chicken breasts into ½" cubes. Sprinkle with chili powder, salt, and pepper and toss to coat. In heavy skillet, heat vegetable oil and add chicken cubes. Cook and stir until chicken is thoroughly cooked, about 4–7 minutes, stirring frequently. Remove chicken from skillet.

2. In medium bowl, combine Muenster cheese, Cheddar cheese, and jalapeño peppers. Make sandwiches using flour tortillas, cheese mixture, and cooked chicken. Cook, one at a time, on heated griddle, turning once,

until tortillas are crisp and cheese is melted, about 4-6 minutes. Cut into quarters and serve immediately.

Calcabacita with Ginger

Calcabacita is Mexican succotash — a combination of squash (or in this case zucchini) and corn. Ginger is the surprise ingredient here; it adds a wonderfully crisp flavor to this smooth and mellow vegetarian main dish.

Serves 6

Ingredients

2 tablespoons olive oil
1 onion, chopped
3 cloves garlic, minced
2 zucchini, sliced thin
2 tomatoes, peeled and chopped
2 cups frozen corn
¼ teaspoon ground ginger
½ teaspoon salt
⅛ teaspoon pepper
½ cup vegetable broth

1. Heat oil in heavy skillet over medium heat. Add onion and garlic; cook until crisp-tender, about 3–4 minutes, stirring frequently. Add zucchini and tomatoes; cook and stir for 2–3 minutes.

2. Add frozen corn, ginger, salt, pepper, and vegetable broth and stir well. Cover pan and simmer for 4–6 minutes until mixture is thoroughly heated and flavors are blended. Serve with hot cooked rice.

Tex-Mex Risotto

Whatever you do, don't rush making risotto or you risk having chewy rice. On the other hand, if you overcook it you end up with mush. Just keep a close eye on it, stir and taste frequently, and you'll end up with Tex-Mex perfection!

Serves 4

Ingredients

1 Anaheim chile
1 onion, chopped
3 cloves garlic, minced
2 tablespoons olive oil
2 tablespoons butter
1 cup Arborio or short-grain rice
4 cups vegetable broth
1 tablespoon lime juice
1 tablespoon chili powder
2 tomatoes, seeded and chopped
½ cup grated Parmesan cheese
1 tablespoon butter

1. Roast the Anaheim chile over a gas flame or under the broiler until skin is blackened. Remove to paper bag and let steam for 10 minutes. Remove the skin with a paper towel; do NOT rinse chile. Remove seeds, chop, and set aside.

2. In heavy skillet, cook onion and garlic in olive oil and 2 tablespoons butter until onion is tender. Add rice; cook and stir for 2–3 minutes until rice is coated with butter mixture. In another saucepan, heat vegetable broth, lime juice, and chili powder until hot; turn off burner.

3. Add vegetable broth mixture, ½ cup at a time, to the rice mixture, cooking and stirring over medium heat. Continue until all the broth is absorbed and the mixture is creamy, about 20-25 minutes total. Add reserved chopped chile, tomatoes, cheese, and butter; cook and stir for 2–3 minutes to melt cheese and butter.

Menu Ideas
Risotto is a classic Italian dish given a Tex-Mex twist with chiles, chili powder, lime juice, and tomatoes. Serve it with some chewy breadsticks or toasted garlic bread, a cool fruit salad dressed with honey and lime juice, and a chocolate ice cream pie for dessert.

Veggie-Heavy Taco Salad

Serve this vegetarian taco salad to your meat-eating friends and see if they even notice what's missing! The flavors meld in such a way and the beans provide heft, so the dish still feels substantial.

Serves 6-8

Ingredients

2 tablespoons olive oil
1 onion, chopped
3 cloves garlic, minced
1 red bell pepper, chopped
1 yellow squash, chopped
2 jalapeño peppers, minced
1 teaspoon cumin
1 tablespoon chili powder
½ teaspoon Tabasco sauce
1 (14-ounce) can diced tomatoes with green chiles, undrained
2 (14-ounce) cans pinto beans, drained
1 cup diced Cheddar cheese
1 (10-ounce) bag mixed salad greens
2 cups slightly crushed tortilla chips
1 cup shredded pepper jack cheese
1 cup salsa
½ cup sour cream

1. In heavy skillet over medium heat, heat olive oil and add onion and garlic. Cook and stir for 4–5 minutes

until crisp-tender. Add red pepper, yellow squash, and jalapeño; cook 2 minutes longer. Add cumin, chili powder, Tabasco sauce, tomatoes, and pinto beans. Simmer mixture, stirring occasionally, for 10 minutes. Remove from heat, sprinkle with Cheddar cheese, and set aside while preparing rest of salad.

2. Place salad greens and crushed tortilla chips on serving plates and top with vegetable mixture. Sprinkle with pepper jack cheese, garnish with salsa and sour cream, and serve.

Make-Ahead Tip
You can make the vegetable mixture ahead of time if you'd like. Prepare it up to the addition of the tomatoes and pinto beans, then cool, cover, and store in the refrigerator. Bring the mixture back to a simmer and continue with the recipe.

Curaçao Margaritas

There's no other liquor that quite matches the electric blue that is curacao! Break out a pitcher of these festive margaritas to add some zing to any gathering.

Serves 8

Ingredients

¼ cup lime juice
Sugar
¾ cup tequila
½ cup blue curaçao
1 cup freshly squeezed lime juice
½ cup triple sec
¾ cup margarita mix
1 cup pear nectar
8 cups crushed ice

1. Dip rim of margarita glasses in the ¼ cup of lime juice and dip into sugar to coat; set aside.

2. In blender or food processor, combine remaining ingredients, including leftover lime juice. Blend or process until mixture is thick and smooth. Pour into prepared glasses and serve.

Tequila Slammer

A staple on any Tex-Mex cocktails menu, this drink is perfect for when you can't decide between a margarita or a tequila, straight up.

Serves 1

Ingredients
1 measure tequila
1 measure lemon-lime beverage
Dash lime juice

In small glass, mix all ingredients. Cover the top of the glass with your hand and slam it down on the bar or table (be careful!). This will make the drink very fizzy; serve immediately.

Rich Mexican Coffee

Mexican coffee can be made into a delicious alcoholic drink by mixing in a bit of Kahlua or white tequila. And to make it really fancy, dollop with fresh whipped cream as well.

Serves 4

Ingredients

½ cup dark-roast coffee grounds
1 teaspoon cinnamon
½ vanilla bean
4 cups cold water
¼ cup chocolate syrup
½ cup sweetened condensed milk
½ cup heavy cream
Dash cinnamon
2 tablespoons powdered sugar

1. In drip coffeemaker, place coffee grounds, cinnamon, and vanilla bean. Add 4 cups cold water and brew. Meanwhile, in small bowl combine chocolate syrup and condensed milk and mix well. Divide syrup mixture among 4 coffee mugs. In small bowl, combine cream, dash cinnamon, and sugar; beat until stiff peaks form.

2. When coffee has finished brewing, pour over syrup mixture in mugs and stir well. Top with flavored whipped cream and serve.

About Mexican-Grown Coffee

Coffee, especially organic coffee, has been a major crop in Mexico since coffee plants arrived from Jamaica in the nineteenth century. Varieties include Arabica and Altura. Most of the organic beans are grown on small farms with high standards, which helps ensure high quality.

Frozen Bananas with Chocolate and Cayenne

If you want to forgo the spice in this, you can easily take out the chili powder and cayenne and instead add a dash of cinnamon and cocoa powder for a totally sweet, creamy, chocolate frozen treat.

Yields 18

Ingredients
4 cups milk
2 (3-ounce) packages instant vanilla pudding mix
3 bananas
1 tablespoon lime juice
¼ teaspoon ground ancho chile powder
⅛ teaspoon cayenne pepper
1 cup frozen whipped topping, thawed
2 cups mini semisweet chocolate chips
18 paper drink cups
18 frozen-dessert sticks

1. In large bowl, combine milk and pudding mixes and beat with wire whisk until thickened. In small bowl, mash bananas with lime juice and stir into pudding mixture. Add chile powder, cayenne pepper, and fold in whipped topping and mini chocolate chips. Divide mixture evenly among paper drink cups.

2. Place drink cups on baking sheet and freeze for 1–2 hours until just firm. Insert frozen-dessert sticks into banana mixture, return to freezer, and freeze for 3–4

hours until frozen solid. Peel away drink cups to serve.

Smooth Mango Pie

Similar in flavor and texture to a cheesecake, this sweetie pie dessert will impress your dinner guests. Serve with some tart raspberries on the side to counter the sweet.

Serves 8

Ingredients

2 cups shortbread cookie crumbs

½ cup shredded coconut

⅓ cup butter, melted

1 (20-ounce) jar mango slices

1 (8-ounce) package cream cheese, softened

1 (14-ounce) can sweetened condensed milk

1 (1-ounce) envelope unflavored gelatin

¼ cup reserved mango juice

2 tablespoons lemon juice

¼ teaspoon salt

½ cup heavy cream

1 teaspoon vanilla

2 tablespoons powdered sugar

1. Preheat oven to 375°F. In medium bowl, combine cookie crumbs, coconut, and melted butter; mix well. Press into bottom and up sides of 9" pie plate. Bake at 375°F for 8–10 minutes until coconut begins to brown; watch carefully. Set aside to cool completely.

2. Drain mango slices, reserving ¼ cup juice; purée mango slices in blender; measure out 1 cup puree. Freeze any remaining puree. In large bowl, beat cream cheese until light and fluffy, then add condensed milk and 1 cup mango puree; beat until smooth.

3. In small microwave-safe bowl, combine reserved ¼ cup mango juice, lemon juice, and unflavored gelatin. Let stand for 5 minutes to soften, then microwave on high power for 20–30 seconds; stir until gelatin is completely dissolved. Fold into mango mixture along with salt. In small bowl, beat cream with vanilla and powdered sugar; fold into mango mixture.

4. Pour mango mixture into cooled pie crust. Cover and refrigerate for 3–4 hours until firm. Garnish with more whipped cream and mint leaves, if desired.

Using Fresh Mangoes
Fresh mangoes can be used in this pie. To prepare a mango, cut the fruit in half, avoiding the pit in the center. Score through the flesh in a checkerboard pattern and push on the skin so it turns inside out and the flesh is exposed. Use a knife to slice the cubes off the skin.

Dulce de Leche

Featuring three types of milk — whole milk, sweetened condensed milk, and heavy whipping cream — this dessert is not for the faint of heart. Translated, it means "sweet of the milk" or "milk candy," and you'll know why once you try it!

Serves 8

Ingredients
1¼ cups flour
1¼ cups sugar
1½ teaspoons baking powder
¼ cup butter, softened
¼ teaspoon salt
6 tablespoons whole milk
1 teaspoon vanilla
2 egg whites
1 (14-ounce) can sweetened condensed milk
1 cup heavy whipping cream
½ cup whole milk
2 tablespoons rum, if desired

1. Preheat oven to 350°F. Grease and flour a 9" round baking pan and line bottom with waxed paper; set aside.

2. In large bowl, combine flour, sugar, and baking powder and mix well. Add butter, salt, milk, and vanilla and beat on low speed until combined. Then

add unbeaten egg whites and beat for 2 minutes on medium speed. Pour batter into prepared pan. Bake at 350°F for 25–35 minutes or until cake is light golden brown and starts to pull away from sides of pan. Cool on wire rack for 15 minutes, then remove from pan, peel off waxed paper, and cool completely on wire rack.

3. Place cake in a deep serving dish with sides and pierce surface of cake with fork. In medium bowl, combine condensed milk, whipping cream, whole milk, and rum; beat well until combined. Slowly pour over cake. Cover and refrigerate cake for 2–4 hours until milk mixture is absorbed. Store covered in refrigerator.

Tex-Mex Chocolate Flan

A classic custardy Tex-Mex dessert, the basis of flan is a rich egg and milk mixture that's baked until set. Carefully follow the instructions for best results!

Serves 8

Ingredients

¾ cup sugar

2 tablespoons water

1 cup whole milk

1 (14-ounce) can sweetened condensed milk

1 vanilla bean

⅓ cup chocolate syrup

2 tablespoons cocoa powder

½ cup semisweet chocolate chips

4 eggs

2 eggs yolks

¼ cup sugar

1. Preheat oven to 325°F. In small heavy saucepan, combine ¾ cup sugar and water. Cook over medium heat, stirring frequently, until sugar melts and turns golden. Watch carefully. When the sugar is completely melted, carefully pour mixture into six 6-ounce custard cups or ramekins that you hold with oven mitts; swirl to coat bottom of cups. Set aside.